Sept. 7, 1975

Dear Greg

I'm very sorry that you were not able to get your (communicators) cuanicaters. maybe next year you mite be able to get your communicatores.

Love Philip

Sept. 7, 1975

Dear Gregory,

have a very Happy Birthday today.

Now you can be baptised. This
is a very important time for you.
I hope you will always remember it.
Also remember the promises you will be
making to Heavenly Father when you
are baptised. Everytime you take the
the Sacrament you are making these
same promises over again. So think about
them every Sunday. Your father and I
love you very much and we are so proud
of you.   Love Always

Mom

Now You Are Eight

Feliz
Cumple Años
Hijo —

Tu padre siempre te quiere mucho. Tu eres diferente que otras personas en el mundo y ha si me gustas. Has crecido muy pronto. Me acuerdo cuando nacistes. Fuistes un muy lindo "bebito". Pero los distes (a tus padres) un susto muy grande - ¿Te acuerdas por que? Dios te ha bendicido mucho - con salud, con familia, y con amor de otros. Da gracias ha Dios todo los dias. El habla con tiene muchas esperanzas y planes para ti. Acuérdate de las el para que te diga cuales son. Acuérdate de las promesas que yo te ha hecho sobre fumar y tomar. Hojala que en dies años yo pueda cumplir con mi promesa.

Con todo mi cariño
Tu padre
H
Septiembe 7, 1975

Now You Are Eight
A Birthday
Book

Edited by Alison M. Abel

Illustrated by Sarah Hale

RAND McNALLY & COMPANY
Chicago · New York · San Francisco

Published in the U.S.A.
by Rand McNally & Company 1973
ISBN 0-528-82195-4

© Ward Lock Limited, London 1973

First published in Great Britain in 1973
by Ward Lock Limited.
116 Baker Street, London, W1M 2BB

Text filmset in 14 pt Apollo
by Yendall & Company Ltd, London

Printed and bound in Belgium
by Casterman S.A., Tournai.

CONTENTS

The Man Who Changed the Weather

Puddleton-on-Sea was usually a quiet, sleepy little fishing village, but today it was all hustle and bustle. Villagers in their Sunday best ran busily to and fro (and hither and thither) though none was too sure why they were running. It just seemed to be the right thing to do on such an important occasion. On the beach stood a red and yellow striped tent with a very important-looking flag flying from its mast. It was the royal flag of King Carbuncle the Third. Today was the King's birthday – the day of the 'Royal Annual Dip in the Sea'.

There was a fanfare of trumpets and the King, dressed in his royal red and yellow striped bathing-suit, stepped out of the royal bathing-hut. The people cheered and the King turned, smiled, waved, and raised his crown to them. He looked very happy. It was well known that King Carbuncle loved his 'Royal Annual Dip in the Sea'. Then he turned toward the sea – and his face fell.

'Prime Minister! Prime Minister!' he shouted. 'What is the meaning of this?'

'The m-meaning of wh-what, your M-majesty?'

The Prime Minister wished his teeth would stop chattering. It was, he thought to himself, unusually cold for the time of year. Very curious! And now, on this day of all days, the King seemed to be upset about something. Even more curious! Or should it be curiouser? He couldn't think properly. He wished he felt warmer.

'Prime Minister!' roared the King, and

the Prime Minister ran as fast as he could across the sand to the King's side.

'Anything the m-m-matter, sire?' he enquired.

'Anything the matter? Anything the matter? I come here in the middle of August for my "Royal Annual Dip in the Sea", and find the sea is frozen solid — and you ask me if anything is the matter!'

The Prime Minister looked at the sea. The King was right — it *was* the middle of August, and the sea *was* frozen solid.

'Oh dear,' he murmured. 'I thought it was unusually cold for the time of year.'

The King looked as if he were going to burst.

'Grrumph, Prime Minister! You are a

'Sire!' One of the King's messengers, Sir Pummystone, a Knight of the Bath, spoke. 'I have recently returned from the North Pole, and there the sun is shining so warmly that the ice is melting!'

'And sire!' Another of the King's messengers, Sir Fishfork of the Household Cavalry, spoke. 'I have recently returned from Africa. There the desert has been flooded and snow has been falling in the jungle!'

'Hot sun at the North Pole, floods in the desert, snow in the jungle,' muttered the Prime Minister. 'Dear, dear, dear — all this is most irregular.'

'Oh Prime Minister, do be quiet!' shouted the King. 'We know it's irregular.

pumpencoop — I mean a coopernimp — dash it, I mean a nincompoop!' And he tried to hit the Prime Minister over the head with his royal water-wings; but he slipped on a frozen rock-pool, and with a clump, bump (and a grrumph), landed heavily on his royal bottom.

The royal party returned speedily to the palace where King Carbuncle summoned all his courtiers before him.

'Go out and search the land far and wide,' he ordered. 'Find out who is responsible for this outrageous state of affairs, and bring him to me.'

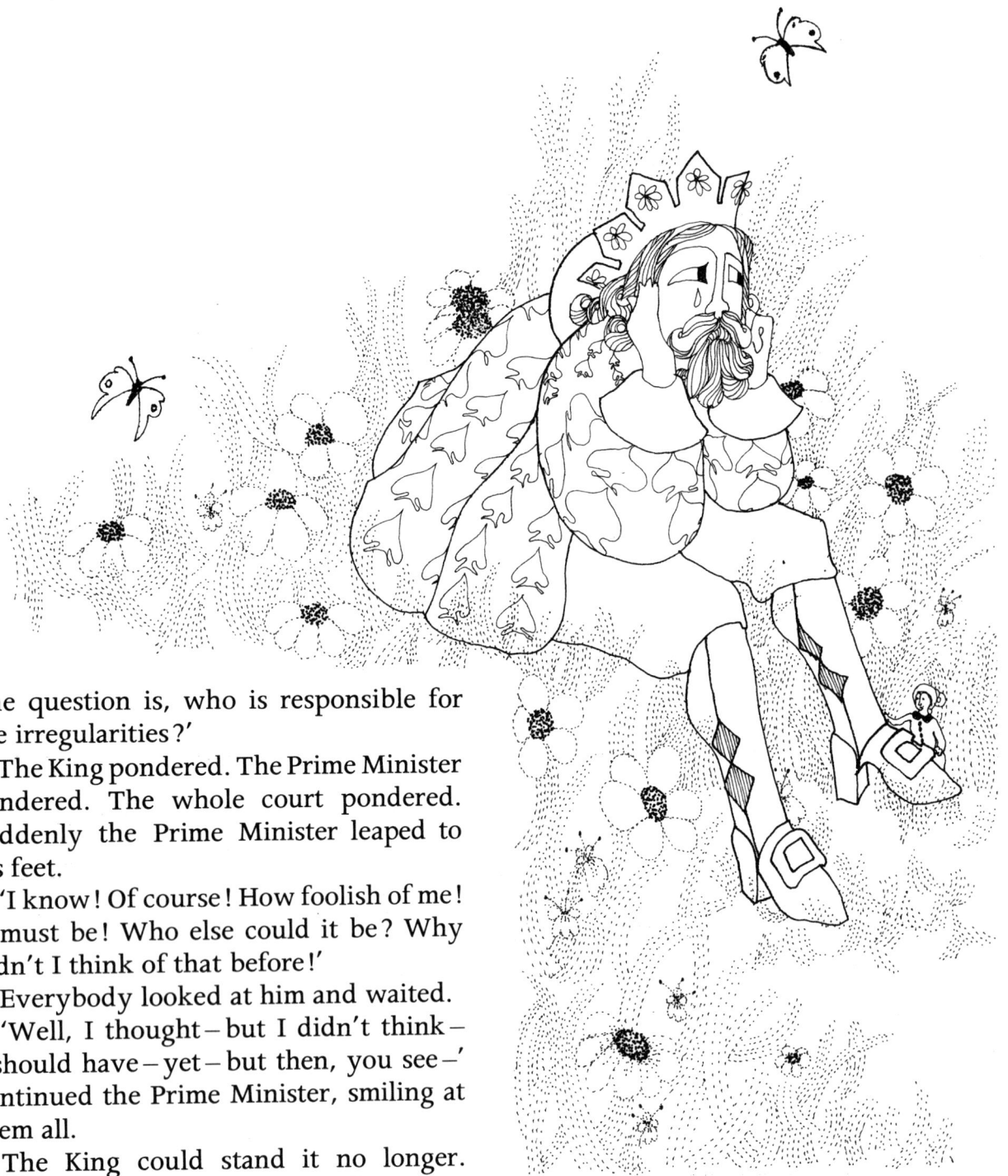

The question is, who is responsible for the irregularities?'

The King pondered. The Prime Minister pondered. The whole court pondered. Suddenly the Prime Minister leaped to his feet.

'I know! Of course! How foolish of me! It must be! Who else could it be? Why didn't I think of that before!'

Everybody looked at him and waited.

'Well, I thought – but I didn't think – I should have – yet – but then, you see –' continued the Prime Minister, smiling at them all.

The King could stand it no longer. 'Prime Minister, if you don't tell us what you are talking about at once, I'll – I'll confiscate your marbles and stop your pocket money for a fortnight. *Who is it?*'

The Prime Minister looked startled. 'Oh, sorry, your Majesty. Didn't I tell you? Why, it's the Weatherman, of course. He's in charge of the weather, and quite clearly he's playing games to amuse

himself. He does get a bit bored, you know, with all this never-ending Spring, Summer, Autumn, Winter, Spring, Summer, Autumn.'

'Prime Minister! Stop that nonsense at once!' ordered the King. 'Lead us to this Weatherman, and I'll have something to say to him.'

The Prime Minister shuffled his feet. 'Ah, that's the problem,' he said weakly. 'No one knows where he lives.'

King Carbuncle the Third stamped his foot. 'Then go and look for him!' he shouted.

And he sent his knights to search the land from top to bottom, from tip to tail, from end to end, to find the Weatherman, and to order him to bring the weather back to normal.

So off they rode. To the North, to the South, to the East, to the West, to the South West, to the North East, and even to the East West East and West East West. Every direction you could think of. But they didn't find the Weatherman. The knights came back one by one, wearily riding their horses through the gates of the palace, without any word of where he might be. Summer was nearly over, and the King was beginning to think he would never have his 'Royal Annual Dip in the Sea'. Some days it would be beautifully sunny; but no sooner had he put on his bathing-suit and picked up his water-wings than the sun would disappear and snow would start to fall. Poor King Carbuncle grew very despondent.

Then one day he went for a walk in the palace gardens to look at the royal flower-beds. This made him feel even more despondent, for the flowers had become so confused by the changes in the weather they had all disappeared underground. The King sat down on a stone and began to cry.

Then he felt a tug at his sleeve.

'Go away,' he said crossly. 'Leave me alone!'

'Now, now, now,' said a quiet, gentle voice. 'That's no way to be talking. Nothing's ever as bad as it seems. Every cloud has a silver staircase.'

'Landing,' corrected the King. 'Anyway, who are you?' He looked left, he

looked right. But he couldn't see anyone. 'More to the point,' he added, 'where are you?'

'Down here on your foot – not everyone's as big as you are, you know.'

The King looked down, and there, sitting on his left shoe, was a little man dressed in a green velvet suit with shiny gold buttons and a big buckle. His eyes were emerald green, and they twinkled as he spoke. 'And as for who I am,' he continued, 'my name is Algernon Herbert Twitchnose, but you can call me Twitch.' And he winked.

But even that did not cheer up King Carbuncle.

'That's very kind of you,' he said as politely as he could. 'Now will you please go away and leave me to be unhappy on my own?'

But the little man would not be dismissed. 'King Carbuncle, this is no way to carry on. You're only upset because the Weatherman is playing tricks with the weather and your knights can't find him, and you've had to do without your "Royal Annual Dip in the Sea". Isn't that so now?'

The King was surprised. 'Yes, you're quite right. But how do you know?'

'Ah,' said Twitch, 'there's lots that I know that I don't tell, and lots that I tell that I don't know.' His eyes twinkled mischievously. 'But you're not to worry any more. I am going to help you.'

'You!' exclaimed the King. 'How can a little fellow like you help when all my royal knights have failed?'

Twitch looked hurt. 'There's nothing wrong with being small,' he said. 'It's being so big and blundering that makes the royal knights miss everything important. You know the old saying: "Empty cabbages make the most sound".'

'Teapots,' King Carbuncle interrupted.

'Quite so, quite so,' said Twitch. 'Empty cabbages make the most teapots. Are you sure? That doesn't sound quite right to me.'

'Oh it doesn't matter, I'm sure you were right the first time,' said the King kindly. 'But how can you help me to find the Weatherman?'

Twitch smiled. 'Well, you see, he's my uncle. He lives in a cottage in Tumbledown Wood. It's very hard to find it if you're big, but I could take you there.'

The King leaped to his feet. 'What are we waiting for? I'll summon the guards and we'll be off.'

But Twitch wasn't in any hurry. 'No need to rush, King Carbuncle. You know the old saying: "More haste, less spaghetti". Now, I think we two should go alone. We don't want the whole world to know where Uncle lives. And please try not to be too angry with him. I know he's been rather naughty, but he doesn't mean any harm, I'm sure. He's a kind old man at heart.'

'Oh . . . grrumph!' said the King, which this time meant that he agreed.

Twitch said it would take them several hours to get to his uncle's cottage, so they asked the royal cook to make a few sandwiches and find a bottle of lemonade, and they had a picnic on the way. Luckily the Weatherman had chosen to make it a sunny winter's sort of day, which was just right for a walk through the woods. When they arrived at the Weatherman's cottage, the King was feeling in very good spirits. He rapped smartly on the cottage door.

'Come in, come in,' called a cheerful voice, and in they went. There, in the middle of a cluttered, jumbly room,

stood an old man with a long white beard and a pointed hat. He was bending over a huge map of the world which was covered with strange signs and lines and writing.

'Now, let me see. What shall I do next? A snowstorm in the Sahara, perhaps; or shall I give everyone at the seaside a snowy summer holiday? Tee-hee-hee, this is fun!' And he tittered mischievously.

The King stepped forward. 'Weatherman, this has gone far enough. Snow in Africa, hot sun at the North Pole, and my "Royal Annual Dip in the Sea" ruined by ice. Why, for two pins I'd have you locked up forever in my deepest, darkest dungeon!'

The Weatherman turned round so fast he nearly tripped over his beard. 'Oh,

your Majesty – oh dear – oh, I am so sorry. I didn't mean – but – oh goodness me ——' And he fell down on his knees, looking very ashamed of himself, and really rather foolish too.

Quickly Twitch interrupted. 'Now, King Carbuncle, remember what you promised. You know what they say: "A friend in need is a friend in a duckpond".'

'In a duckpond?' exclaimed the King, quite forgetting the Weatherman for the moment. 'Good gracious, Twitch, you do say the most ridiculous things!'

He started to laugh. Then Twitch began to laugh with him. And then the Weatherman joined in too, and soon all three were rolling about the cottage floor, clutching their stomachs and giggling helplessly.

'Now look here, Weatherman,' the

11

King said as he recovered his Royal dignity and his crown, which had fallen off when he was laughing, 'this really hasn't been good enough, all this playing about with the weather. You must promise to behave yourself in future, or you'll be in trouble.'

'Oh, I will, I will,' the old man promised.

'Well, just to be on the safe side, I'm going to leave your nephew, Twitch, here to keep a weather-eye on you. Twitch, I hereby appoint you Assistant Royal Weatherman!'

Twitch agreed to help, and the Weatherman promised to be good. 'And your Majesty,' he called, as King Carbuncle turned to go, 'if you want to take your "Royal Annual Dip in the Sea" tomorrow, I'll make sure it's a really beautiful sunny day.'

And sure enough, the next day the weather was beautiful, and King Carbuncle the Third had a lovely dip in the sea. And from that day on the Weatherman did behave himself most of the time, and the snow came in winter, and the hot sun in summer, just as it had always done. But if one summer's day you find it's suddenly grown quite cold, or if one winter's day it is unusually warm, you'll know that, just for a minute, he has forgotten his promise, and is enjoying himself playing tricks with the weather again.

Games
to Play at Parties

Having a party? It's a good idea to plan ahead the games you can play. Here are some which you and your friends are sure to enjoy.

FISH RACE

You can play this game in a large room, or even out in the yard if it is not too windy. Before the party cut out fish from tissue paper. Have ready some plates, and some magazines or folded newspapers. To play the game, space out the plates at one end of the room. The players stand in a row at the other end, each with a fish on the floor in front of him. By hitting the magazines on the floor behind the fish the players can flip them along toward the plates. The idea is to get the fish on to the plates without touching them with the magazine. The one who gets his fish on the plate first is the winner.

I PACKED MY BAG

This is a good game for testing your memory. The players sit in a circle on the floor. The first one starts by saying: 'I packed my bag and in it I put . . .' and adds whatever he likes – say a brush. The player to his right then says: 'I packed my bag and in it I put a brush and a . . .' and adds what he would pack – perhaps a roller-skate. The game goes on round and round the circle, each player adding a new thing to pack in the bag. When someone forgets what comes next or makes a mistake, he drops out of the game. The last player left is the winner.

SPINNING THE PLATE

The guests stand in a ring and count off so that each has a number. One player is chosen as the spinner. He stands in the middle of the ring holding a large plastic or tin plate. As he spins the plate he calls out a number. The player whose number has been called must run into the ring and catch the plate before it drops. If he catches it in time he becomes the new spinner, and the first spinner joins the ring.

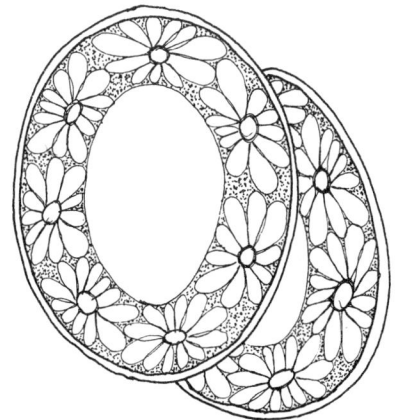

13

Lions in Longships

Do you know who first discovered America? Once people believed that it was Christopher Columbus. Now we know that five hundred years before Columbus the Vikings sailed to America from Greenland.

The first Vikings came from Scandinavia. In those days it was a bleak, wild land where wolves roamed and only the hardiest people could live. Every spring these pirates set sail in their 'longships'. They began by invading only small islands, but later they attacked many parts of Europe far from their homeland.

It must have been a wonderful – and terrifying – sight to see the Viking longships sailing across the seas. Each one had a figurehead carved and painted in the

14

shape of a fierce animal—perhaps a dragon, a bull, or a bear. The mast was planted amidships, and the sails, which were square, were often vividly striped. Sometimes the sails were lined with fur. The vanes at the top of the masts were shaped and decorated to look like birds. Along the gunwales the shields of the warriors overlapped each other like fish scales. When the sea was rough these shields kept the water from washing overboard.

The oarsmen sat in the middle section of the longship on wooden chests in which they kept their belongings. At the fore end, which was raised high, stood the best warriors. The Viking chief stood on another raised deck at the stern. From here he could direct the ship and give orders to the warriors when the fighting began.

Sometimes, when a Viking chief died, he was buried in his longship under a mound of earth. Some of these buried ships have been found by archaeologists. One, which is now in a museum in Oslo, is seventy-eight feet long and just under seventeen feet wide across its broadest point. It is made out of thirty-two over-lapping planks riveted together with iron, and has sixteen oars at each side. After this ship was found, a replica was made and sailed across the Atlantic to America. At times it reached a speed of ten knots.

The most terrifying Vikings of all were the Jomsburgers. Their stronghold was at the mouth of the Oder river. Here they kept their booty and spent the winters refitting their ships. No man could join the Jomsburgers if he had ever been beaten in a fight. When they went to war the Jomsburgers dressed themselves in jerkins of hardened deerskin. To frighten their enemies they put wolves' heads over their iron helmets. Some of them carried double-headed axes with sharp spikes on five-foot long handles.

The Vikings planned most of their invasions so that they arrived in their chosen country soon after harvest-time, when the barns were full. They came at night, so that no one would be prepared for them, and when they were near land they lowered their sails and masts so they should not be seen. Then the Vikings would hide their glinting helmets and armor under dark, hooded cloaks, put on sheepskin overshoes so that they would make no noise when they reached land, and wind strips of sheepskin round the

blades of the oars to muffle the sound as they rowed to the shore.

The Vikings were very good horsemen as well as fine sailors. As soon as they had reached dry land and beached their ships they would search round for horses to steal. Then, riding swiftly across the land, they would plunder the farms and villages, stealing sheep, fodder, and anything else they could find. When at last they sailed away, each longship had trailing behind it the carcasses of sheep, hung into the sea from ropes and chains so that the meat would be preserved in the salt.

As time passed, instead of returning home when winter came, more and more Vikings settled in the countries they plundered. Some settled in England and Ireland. Others went up the Seine in France to Rouen and took over what is now Normandy, which means 'the land of the men from the North'. Others sailed farther south and invaded Spain and Morocco, and some even found their way to Constantinople. Russia is named after the Swedish Vikings known as the 'Rus' who colonized Novgorod in 862.

The most adventurous Vikings were those who came from Norway. They were led by Eric the Red, who discovered Iceland. Later he sailed to another land, where the grass was good for grazing cattle. So he called this place 'Greenland'. In 986 more Vikings set sail to join Eric the Red and his men in Greenland. One of their ships was driven off course on its way, and the men who sailed in this ship were the first to sight North America – though they only saw it in the distance, and did not land there.

About fourteen years later Eric the Red's son, Leif the Lucky, decided to sail westward from Greenland and see for himself this land that had been sighted. He and his men landed first in Labrador. Then they followed the coastline south till they reached what is now New

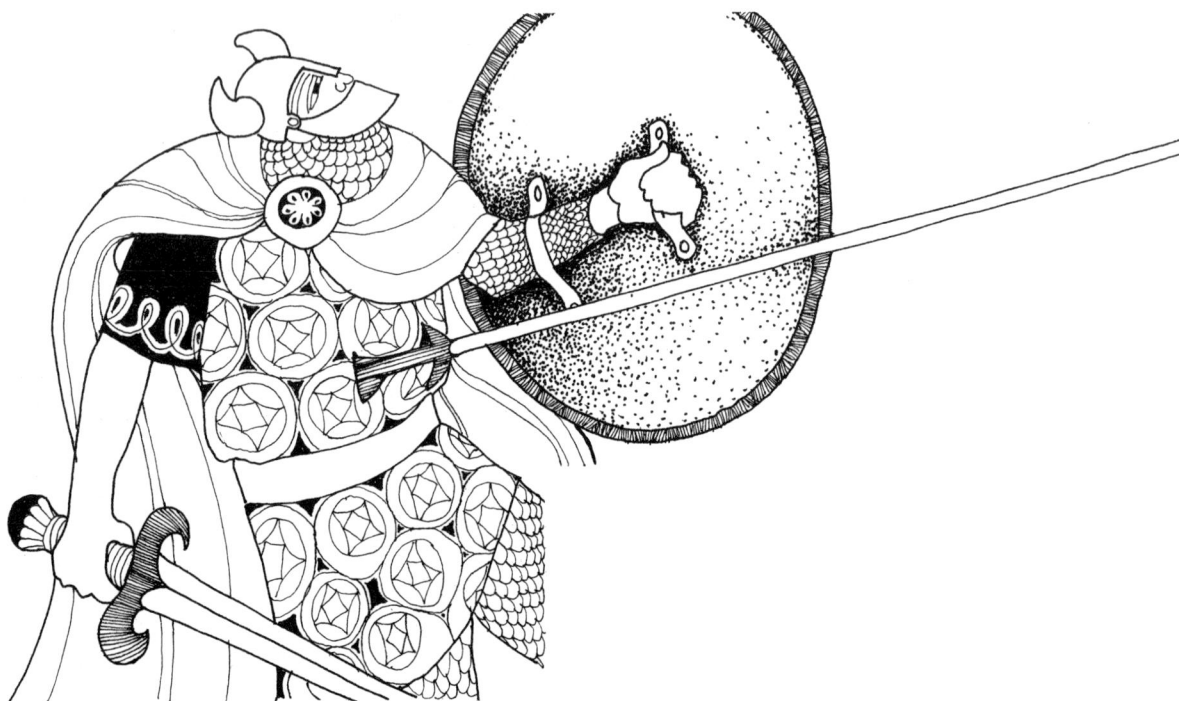

16

England. Here they were amazed to see such rich and fertile land. Leif was particularly struck by what he called 'wine berries', so he named the country 'Vinland'. When Leif and his men returned to Greenland, they told the other Vikings about the wine berries and some of them decided they would go and live in this rich new country. But after a few years they began drifting back again, complaining that they had had few of the wine feasts promised them.

The early Vikings followed a pagan religion, and they believed that to fight, and to die fighting, was a glorious thing. When the Vikings sat round their camp-fires they would listen to harpists playing and singing the praises of fallen heroes, and urging the men to follow the brave example of those killed in battle. They believed that if they died in battle they would go straight to their Heaven, Valhalla. There, with Odin and the other Gods, they would live forever, feasting all night long in celebration of the great battles they had won.

The King With the Golden Touch

Long, long ago, in a far off sunny country, lived a king called Midas. He was very rich, and he loved gold. He would sit for hours counting his money, gloating as the piles of gold coins rose higher and higher. He longed to fill his palace with treasures, all of solid gold. And did he spend anything on other people, or give money away to the poor? Never!

One day as he sat counting his money he heard the sound of shouts and laughter. Looking up, he saw the peasants who worked in his gardens and orchards coming into the courtyard. They were carrying Silenus, a bewildered, fat old satyr. He had a man's head and body, but the hairy legs of a goat. Chains of flowers were twined round him. He had drunk too much wine and lost his way – and not only his way, but also the wild ass which carried him everywhere.

At last Silenus had stumbled into the palace gardens and fallen into a deep sleep. There the peasants had found him. Satyrs, they told one another, lived in woods, not gardens. So with much joking about this odd creature they had brought him to Midas.

Midas knew that Silenus was the friend of Bacchus, the god of wine and pleasure. He knew too that Bacchus had power to grant men's wishes. So instead of joining in the laughter he made the fat old man welcome. And after a few days Midas set out with him to find Bacchus.

They rode through the woods and at last saw the god lying on a flowery bank, with vine leaves in his hair and a bunch of grapes in his hands.

Bacchus was very glad to see Silenus, whose ass had come back to the woods without its master.

'You have been kind to Silenus,' said Bacchus. 'Tell me, Midas, what I can do for you in return?'

King Midas' heart beat faster. This was what he had hoped for.

'I have some gold, some treasures,' he said, 'but not enough. Give me, Bacchus,

the power to turn everything I touch into gold.'

Bacchus hesitated. He saw the danger in such a wish. But he saw too the greedy look in the King's eyes. So he laughed, and granted the wish.

Midas went home full of joy. To test whether Bacchus had really given him this power he touched a twig. At once its brown bark and green leaves stiffened and changed color. Midas looked with delight at the gleaming gold. His wish had come true! He broke off the twig and twirled it in his fingers to make it glitter and flash in the sunlight.

He picked up a stone. Instantly that too was shining gold. He put it into his pocket. The soft folds of his robes felt strange. He looked down: they too were gleaming gold. He went through a field of corn, and plucked one of the ears; again, it turned to gold. In his own orchards and gardens the apples and roses he picked became gold.

Laden with these new treasures King Midas reached his palace. His courtiers gaped in astonishment as he went up the steps. The sun reflecting from his robes dazzled their eyes. At the top of the great staircase the King made a gleaming heap of all that he carried. Then he put his hands on a pillar and the courtiers saw the pillar change from stone to solid gold.

King Midas wanted everyone to admire and envy his new magical powers. So he invited all his neighbors to a costly feast. They came full of curiosity, for they had heard strange rumors of the riches piling up in the palace.

When the guests were all seated King Midas came into the banqueting hall and walked to the head of the table. His heavy robes of gold made a strange jingling sound as he moved.

At first Midas touched nothing. He watched his guests enjoying the rich food. Then he stretched out his hand to a crystal goblet of wine. The guests stopped eating and watched him. The King was looking forward to seeing their surprise when the crystal turned to gold.

And turn it did—but so did the wine as it touched his lips! He tried to eat, but everything—savory meat pies, cakes heaped high with cream, strange exotic fruits—turned to gold. Thirsty, hungry and angry, King Midas rose and hurried from the table.

His children came running to meet him. Without thinking, he picked up the youngest child—and found himself holding a golden statue!

King Midas wept all night as he lay on his hard golden bed. At dawn he hurried from the palace to the wood where Bacchus lived, and there he told his troubles. He begged the god to take this terrible power from him. Bacchus was a mischievous god, but now he was sorry for Midas. He told him to go to the source of a river and wash himself in the water. Midas ran to a spring bubbling from a rock. He leaped into the cool water—and the spell was broken!

The King touched the grass at the waterside. It stayed green. He ran his fingers over some flowers. They kept their bright colors. Then full of joy and relief he hurried home. There, instead of a golden statue, he saw his youngest child playing happily in the courtyard.

King Midas was a changed man. He never again counted his money, nor could he ever look on gold without remembering his greed and folly.

20

TRAVELLING ON A CUSHION

Do you remember the story from the *Arabian Nights* of the prince who flew on a magic carpet? We all know this is just make-believe; but flying carpets seem nearer reality when you think of the hovercraft.

These wonderful machines can move across land and sea, hovering a few inches above the surface. Of course, it isn't magic that keeps them above the ground, but a cushion of air. A fan driven by a powerful engine sucks the air into a funnel in the center of the hovercraft. The air is then forced out through jets underneath the craft to form the cushion.

The invention of the hovercraft by Sir Christopher Cockerell in the nineteen fifties was a big step forward in the history of transport. Because hovercraft move above the level of the ground they can travel safely over surfaces which would otherwise be impossible. They have been used along parts of the Amazon and Orinoco rivers, for instance, where rapids might capsize a boat and batter it to pieces. Men have also used hovercraft to cross vast swamps and the sandy deserts of Africa where in wheeled vehicles they would soon be in trouble.

Hovercraft can settle on any flattish surface. For this reason they are especially useful for carrying passengers and freight wherever ships, cars and planes find it difficult to travel.

MAGIC TRICKS

You will amaze and amuse your friends with these tricks. Practice them first so that you are really expert. Then you will be the top entertainer at any party!

THE MAGIC PENCIL

Perhaps no one will believe you when you tell them you have a magic pencil. But they may change their minds when you show them how you can fold the pencil inside a piece of paper and then, without touching it, make it appear again on the outside.

Put the sheet of paper on a flat surface, with the pencil in the middle (picture 1). Fold the paper over the pencil so that the top edge overlaps the bottom edge by about an inch (picture 2). Now roll up the paper tightly from the fold, with the pencil still inside (picture 3). When the bottom edge flips over the roll (picture 4) hold it down with one hand and quickly unroll the paper. There is the pencil, on the outside of the folded paper (picture 5). (Be careful not to roll the paper so far that both edges flip over.)

FIND THE ANIMAL

For this trick you will need a sheet of paper and a hat.

Give the paper to one of your friends and ask him to fold it into three equal sections (picture 1). Tell him to draw a bird in the top section, an animal in the middle section, and a fish in the bottom section (picture 2). Now ask your friend to tear the paper into three pieces along the folds (picture 3) and to fold each piece in half to hide what he has drawn. Hold out the hat for him to drop in the folded pieces of paper.

Tell your friends that, without looking, you will find the piece of paper on which is the picture of the animal. Put your hand in the hat and feel the edges of the pieces of paper. The one with the two rough edges will be the one on which the animal is drawn. Take it out of the hat, unfold it, and you can say which animal your friend chose to draw!

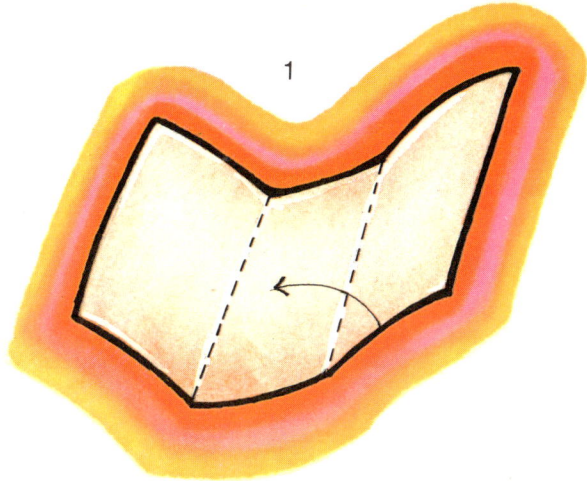

The Magic Thread

There was once a boy called Peter who lived with his widowed mother in a little house at the edge of a village. Peter was good at helping his mother, and he was strong and clever. But he did not like going to school. He would sit in the class-room dreaming of the holidays, or the time when he would be grown up. Then he would be a carpenter, as his father had been.

What Peter did enjoy was wandering in the woods near the village, thinking about the time when he would be a grown man. Of course he often played with his friends too. His closest friend was a little girl called Lisa. Often when she came to play with him Peter would think: 'If only I were grown up, then I could marry Lisa.'

Peter's birthday was in the summer, and on that day Lisa was coming to play with him. In the morning he decided to go for a walk in the woods while he waited for his friend to come.

He wandered through the trees for more than an hour, thinking how nice it was to be one year older – and wishing already that his next birthday would come. Then he began to feel tired; so he lay down in a clearing in the warm sun. Soon he was asleep.

He slept all morning and into the afternoon. Then he was wakened by the

sound of someone calling his name. Peter opened his eyes and stared in surprise. Before him stood a little old woman. She was oddly dressed, and had a strange light in her eye. But she smiled at him in a friendly way.

'Oh Peter,' she said. 'Whatever the time, it is never the right time for you, is it? I have often heard you wishing your days away. Never mind, I've brought a special birthday present for you. Look!'

She showed Peter a little silver ball. From a small hole in the ball came the end of a very fine gold thread.

'This is the thread of your life,' went on the old woman. 'If you want the time to pass quickly, just pull the thread. But if you want it to take as long as it does for other people, then you must leave it alone. Now let me give you a word of warning. Don't pull the thread too hard or too often. You can never push it back once it is pulled out. It just disappears like smoke. And never tell anyone that you have this, for on that day you will die. Now tell me, Peter, do you want the magic ball?'

Peter looked at the woman wonderingly. He had never dreamed of such a wonderful thing.

'Yes, please!' he cried. 'Please give it to me.'

He took the silver ball in his hand, and

when he looked up the old woman had gone. Then Peter leaped to his feet and ran back home through the woods. He was just in time to see Lisa going through the garden gate.

That night, as he lay in bed, Peter wondered whether he should pull out enough of the thread to make him grown up. But he remembered the old woman's warning, and so he left it alone.

The next day, at school, his teacher scolded him for not paying attention. Then Peter decided the time had come to try out his magic ball. Very carefully he pulled the thread – just a little – and it was time to go home.

After that Peter had a wonderful time. He hardly ever went to school. As soon as the time for school to start came he pulled the thread and it was vacation-time again. But one day he thought to himself: 'I'm getting rather bored with these endless

vacations. If I were grown up I could learn my trade, and then I could marry Lisa.'

So that night Peter took out the magic ball from the drawer where he had hidden it, and pulled the thread very hard. Next morning he awoke to find that many years had passed and he was now a grown man.

As soon as he was dressed and had eaten his breakfast he went to see Lisa. She came running to meet him, calling:

'Oh Peter, now we have only six weeks to wait for our wedding!'

So they were married, and everything went smoothly for a few months until Lisa told him that they were going to have a child. Peter could hardly wait for this, so every day he pulled the thread a little. At last the child was born, and Peter was full of joy. But he could not bear it when the baby cried or was ill, so he went on pulling the thread to make these times pass, too.

As the child grew, Peter became more and more content. But then he and Lisa had more children. They were lively and mischievous, and always needing new clothes and more food. Sometimes even Lisa said they were too much for her. At last Peter decided that it would be better if the children were grown up and could help him with his work. So once again he gave the thread a hard tug and the years passed in a flash. Now his children had all left home, and his sons were working as carpenters with him. By this time Peter had silver hairs on his head, and he realized the magic thread would not last forever.

So Peter's life passed more and more quickly. When times were hard he could pull the thread, but more troubles always followed. However many times he pulled the thread, life was never perfect. Then, as he grew older, his work became too much for him. One day he went to his work-room and told his sons to carry on without him. He was too old and tired to work.

Now Peter could spend his days sitting in the doorway of his cottage, smoking his pipe and day-dreaming. But he did not often dream of the future, for he knew that the end of his life was not far

away. Instead, he spent his time remembering the past. But poor Peter! He didn't have many memories of the past at all. His life had passed so quickly, and all the events had come so thick and fast, that it was difficult to remember them. He soon became bored with sitting at the door of the cottage. Then one day he had an idea. He would go for a walk in the woods, where he had not been for many years.

Now that he was old he couldn't walk as far or as fast as when he was a child; but he managed to reach the woods. Then he sat down to rest on an old tree stump. Soon he was fast asleep.

After a while he heard a voice calling his name. He opened his eyes and blinked. Standing before him was the old woman he had met so long ago, looking just the same and not a day older.

'Now, Peter,' she said. 'Have you had a good life? Have you been happy?'

'Well,' said Peter. 'Your little magic ball is wonderful. I've not had to put up with many troubles. But the time has passed so quickly. Now my life is nearing its end, I wish I had not pulled the thread so often. To tell you the truth, your gift has not brought me much happiness.'

'Well!' cried the old woman. 'I must say you're not very grateful. But since you have not been happy with your life, I will grant you one wish. What would you like most of all, Peter?'

Peter thought for a few minutes. Then he said: 'I should like to live my life all over again, without the magic ball. If I had it, I know I should pull the thread too often. Now I want to live like other people.'

The old woman smiled.

'I will grant your wish,' she said. 'If that is really what you want, then give me back my silver ball.'

As soon as Peter had given her the ball he fell once more into a deep sleep. When he awoke he found he was in his own bed in the little cottage, and his mother was sitting beside him.

'So you are awake at last!' she cried.

'Where am I?' asked Peter, looking round the room in bewilderment.

'At home, of course,' replied his mother. 'You have had a bad fever. You stayed out in the sun too long. You must have had terrible dreams. You were always talking about a magic ball and your life's thread.'

'So I'm not an old man?' asked Peter.

'No,' laughed his mother.

Peter leaped out of bed and flung his arms round her neck.

'And Lisa is not an old woman?'

'Of course not!' exclaimed his mother. 'She's sitting in the kitchen, waiting to see you.' And she called: 'Lisa!'

Lisa came running into the room.

'Oh Lisa,' cried Peter. 'I am quite well now. Tomorrow morning we'll go to school together. And one day you and I will be married. I can hardly wait!'

Then, as Peter reached out his hand to Lisa, he gave a gasp of surprise; for clinging to his sleeve was a tiny piece of golden thread.

IN THE DAYS OF THE DRAGONS

Of course, you don't believe in dragons—especially the fire-eating sort which breathe flames. Yet it is perfectly true that the world was inhabited by giant dragons around two hundred million years ago. Although they did not actually breathe fire, they were just as fearsome as any of the dragons in the fairy stories.

You may well wonder how we know, for there were no human beings alive at that time. Well, one day, only a hundred and fifty years ago, an English doctor called Gideon Algernon Mantell drove off on his rounds from the country town of Lewes, in Sussex. His wife went with him, for the ride, and it was really her sharp eyes that spotted the first clue to the dragons.

While the doctor was visiting a patient she went for a short stroll. Suddenly she caught the glint of something shining in a heap of broken rock by the roadside. She went over for a closer look and found an enormous old tooth, turned to stone, or 'fossilized'. She took it to show the doctor. He thought it must have belonged to a great reptile unlike anything alive today.

He then made several expeditions to look for buried teeth and bones, and when some more turned up in a quarry in Kent he was able to describe a giant extinct reptile which he called an 'Iguanodon'. It must have stood upright on its hind legs, because its fore legs were quite tiny, and that made it about fourteen feet tall. It had a powerful tail, like a crocodile's, eleven feet long. It could easily have poked its snout, which was about a yard long, into the bedroom windows of a two-story house. The Iguanodon was a vegetable-eater, or 'vegetarian', and it could browse off the foliage of quite tall trees. Not much of a dragon, you think? But it certainly looked like one.

30

While Dr. Mantell was studying the Iguanodon, some more huge bones turned up in Oxfordshire and were examined by Dean Buckland. These belonged to an even bigger creature, and this was indeed a dragon of the most terrible kind imaginable.

Picture a large crocodile, but with shorter and thicker jaws, measuring thirty feet from snout to tail. Now perch it on the top of two enormous hind legs, ten feet high! Its arms and hands were small but powerful, and were armed with long claws. It had long rows of teeth like sharp-pointed saws, and it hunted smaller animals, chasing them at great speed.

Dean Buckland named it 'Megalosaurus', which means 'great lizard'.

The tracks of dinosaurs were found in America in 1835, but they were thought to belong to giant birds until some bones turned up in 1856. Soon afterward several large deposits of mixed dinosaur bones were found. Many people came to dig in these 'dinosaur mines'. In Montana, Edward Drinker Cope was digging under the very nose of the Sioux Chief Sitting Bull, almost immediately after the Indian chief's victory over General Custer at Little Big Horn. Since that time large numbers of dinosaur bones have been discovered, particularly in the area now known as Dinosaur National Monument in Colorado and Utah.

These discoveries of pre-historic reptiles were very exciting, and since the middle of the nineteenth century expeditions have been sent all over the world to find the bones and teeth of these reptiles which once dominated the earth. Sir Richard Owen called them 'Dinosaurs', which means 'terrible lizards', but it turned out that there were two main groups. One, to which the Iguanodon belongs, left three-toed footprints, like giant birds, and these were vegetarians.

Some dinosaurs walked on all fours and were very heavily armored with plates of bone, long sharp spines and horns. They were like armored cars or tanks, with legs instead of wheels. Though they could not have moved very quickly, some, such as the 'Stegosaurus', could easily have pushed over a small house. One of the horned dinosaurs was the 'Triceratops', which was thirty feet long and had three horns and a huge bony 'frill' to protect its neck.

Triceratops had a hooked beak like a

parrot's, as well as rows of powerful teeth. But other members of this group had beaks like a duck's, and others again – the 'Hadrosaurus' – had as many as five hundred teeth in each jaw, making two thousand teeth in all! They were tightly packed, and their surfaces looked like the pieces in an inlaid mosaic floor.

The other main group of dinosaurs included flesh-eating dragons like the Megalosaurus and the even more terrible 'Tyrannosaurus', which was fifty feet long, had sharp teeth more than four inches long, and could probably stride after you at a speed of forty miles an hour! This group also contained the largest land animals that have ever existed. Some of them must have weighed more than thirty tons – as much as seven elephants!

These monsters, which were vegetarians, had an enormous bulky body, with a very long, snake-like neck and tail. Some were as much as a hundred feet long, and they stood up to twenty feet high at the rump. Their thigh-bones were seven feet long and as thick as tree-trunks. Their heads, on the other hand, were quite small, and they had very small brains. The 'Diplodocus', for example, was often sixty-five feet long, but its head measured only two feet. Its brain, which was scarcely larger than a hen's egg, was much too far away from the tail to control it properly, so there was a sort of secondary brain in the hind-quarters to look after the rear end.

These huge dinosaurs were so heavy that they probably lived for most of the time in large lakes and rivers where their bodies would be buoyed up by the water. Being reptiles, you would expect them to lay eggs, and, sure enough, dinosaurs' eggs have been found as fossils in Central Asia and elsewhere. Sometimes the skeleton of a young dinosaur is preserved inside an unhatched egg.

There were small dinosaurs as well as giant ones, and some were no bigger than modern lizards, but they have left no descendants on earth today. All the dinosaurs died out about sixty million years ago.

DO YOU BELIEVE?

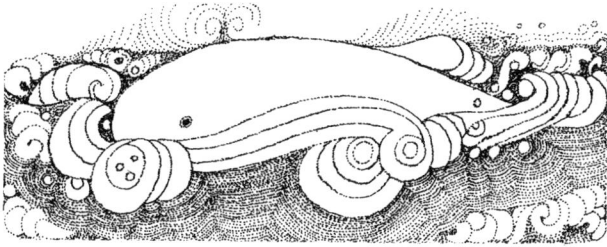

Here are some surprising facts with which you can amaze your friends.

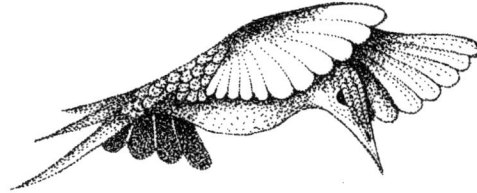

The largest and heaviest animal in the world is the blue whale. The biggest ever found, in the South Shetlands in 1926, was 106 feet long.

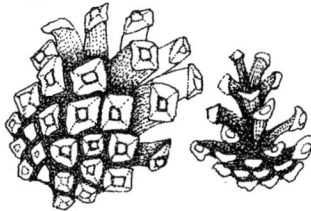

The oldest living tree on record is about 4,900 years old. It is a bristlecone pine growing on the Wheeler Peak in Eastern Nevada, U.S.A.

The longest sausage ever recorded was 3,124 feet long. It was made in 1966 by 30 butchers in Lincolnshire, England.

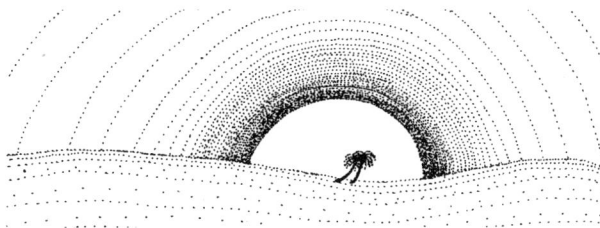

The driest place in the world is Calama, in the Atacama Desert in South America. There is no record of it ever having rained there.

The smallest bird in the world is the male bee hummingbird which is found in Cuba. With its wings spread, it measures $1\frac{1}{2}$ inches from tip to tip. It weighs only $\frac{1}{18}$ of an ounce.

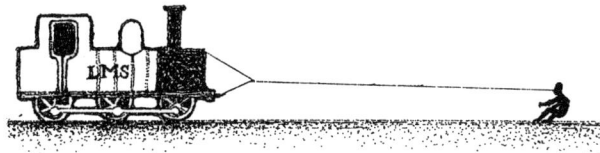

The man with the strongest teeth in the world is John Massis of Belgium. He has pulled a 36-ton train along rails with a bit held between his teeth.

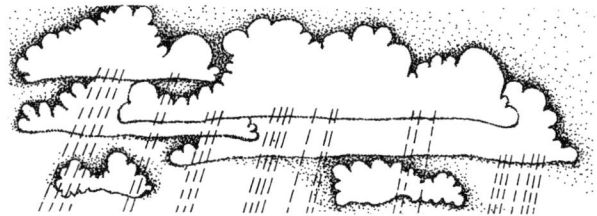

The rainiest place in the world is Bahia Felix, in Chile, where it rains an average 325 days of the year. In 1916 there were 348 days of rain recorded – in other words there were only eighteen days in the year when it didn't rain! (Remember, 1916 was a leap-year.)

Bukolla the Cow

An old man and woman and their only son were once living in a little hut not far from the sea. The old man went out fishing every morning, unless there was a storm at sea. His son Erik would row out to take him his dinner so that he could fish all day long. They always had fish to eat, and what they didn't eat the old man sold in the town.

They also had Bukolla. She was their cow, and she was a magic cow. Erik looked after her. He milked her three times a day, and every time she gave forty pints of the finest milk. The old man sold the milk in the town with the fish to buy bread and other things.

But one day a terrible thing happened. When Erik went to the cowshed in the morning Bukolla was gone.

'You must find her,' said his father and mother. 'You must go out and search until you find her. If you can't, we shall starve.'

'I will go,' said Erik.

He put on a new pair of shoes made of shark-skin, and put some bread and dried fish in his wallet, and set out.

'The trolls must have taken her,' he said to himself.

Now trolls were fearsome creatures who lived in caves in the mountains and ate human beings when they could catch them. Some of them were giants and some were dwarfs. Erik was afraid of the trolls, but he was a brave lad.

'I will go to the mountains where the trolls live,' he said.

He walked and walked until he came to a green hillock. 'Here I will have my breakfast,' he said to himself, and he sat down and ate some of his bread and fish. Then he called at the top of his voice, 'Bellow, Bukolla, so that I can find you. Bellow, Bukolla!'

He listened and listened, but there was no answer, so he set off again toward the mountains.

He walked and walked until he came to another green hillock. 'I'll have my dinner here,' he said to himself, and when he had finished he called, 'Bellow, Bukolla! Bellow, Bukolla!'

This time there was an answering bellow, far away.

'She's in the mountains,' said Erik, so he went on walking.

At last he came to a great rock, and he cried again, 'Bellow, my Bukolla, bellow!'

This time the answering bellow was near at hand. Erik walked along the rock until he came to a large cave.

'This must be a troll's cave,' he thought.

He peered round the edge of the rock. He could not see any trolls, so he went

inside. There was a fire burning, and flat-bread baking on a broad stone in front of it, and meat stewing in an iron pot over it. The stew smelled delicious, and by this time Erik was hungry again. But he would not steal the food. He searched around until he found a small side cave, and there was Bukolla, chained up under a sloping rock.

She bellowed with joy, and Erik ran up to her and hugged her. Quickly he set her free and they hurried out of the cave and down the mountainside.

Bukolla and Erik were halfway home when they heard a terrible noise behind them. They looked round and saw two giant troll women striding after them.

'They'll catch us in no time,' cried Erik. 'What can we do?'

'Pull a hair from my tail and throw it on the ground,' said Bukolla.

Erik did so. Then Bukolla said to the hair, 'I wish you and magic you to become a river so wide that only a flying bird can cross it.'

At once there was a broad river rushing along between them and the trolls. They hurried on.

When the trolls came to the bank the mother-troll said to her daughter, 'This shall not stop us. Run home at once and bring your father's bull.'

Off went the younger troll, and in no time she came galloping back on a black bull, so gigantic that it made the earth shake.

The bull drank up the river water until he and the trolls could wade across. Then on they went after Erik and Bukolla.

Erik looked back. 'They are coming,' he cried. 'What can we do now?'

'Pull a hair from my tail and throw it on the ground,' said Bukolla.

Erik did so, and Bukolla said, 'Hair, I wish you and magic you to become so great a fire that only flying birds can cross it.'

At once a great fire raged across the country, blazing and roaring like a furnace. The trolls could not pass it, but the mother-troll growled, 'Bull, bull, put it out.'

The bull spat out the river water it had drunk in a great flood, until there was nothing left of the fire but black ashes. Then on they went in chase of Erik and Bukolla.

When Erik felt the ground shaking under the hoofs of the giant bull, he stopped and looked back in fear.

'What shall we do now, my Bukolla?' he cried.

'Pull a hair from my tail,' answered Bukolla, 'and throw it on the ground.'

Then she said to the hair, 'I wish you and magic you to become a mountain so great that only a flying bird can pass it.'

No sooner said than done. There was the mountain, so high that its top was hidden in the clouds. Erik and Bukolla hurried on.

'This shall not stop us,' howled the mother-troll. 'Daughter, bring me your father's boring-iron.'

The younger troll galloped off on the black bull and in no time at all she was back with the boring-iron.

'Aha,' growled the mother-troll, 'now we shall have them!'

She worked so hard at the mountain that in a few minutes the iron had gone right through it. The mother-troll pulled it out and looked through the hole. She saw Erik and Bukolla disappearing in the distance.

'They shall not get away!' she screamed in fury, and flung herself into the hole. But it was too small. She stuck fast, and nothing her daughter could do would get her out, so she must be there still.

Erik and Bukolla reached home safely and the mother, the father, the son and the cow were all happy together once again.

The Prince Escapes

John Cameron crouched in the heather on the hill above Glenpean and scanned the rough mountain road. That was the way the Redcoats would come, riding from Fort William. They were hunting for Prince Charles Stuart. The Prince, with a few horsemen, was at the door of John's father's farm. John was only eight years old, but he had understood what the Prince had told his father. There had been a terrible battle at a place called Culloden, and the Prince had lost. He had ridden hard all night to escape the Redcoat soldiers who were hunting for him. John's father had turned sharply to John when he heard this. 'Get you up the hill,' he had said. 'Keep a watch for any soldiers turning up the glen.' He had told the horsemen, 'His eyes are keen. He'll see them afar off.'

So the Prince's safety depended on John. The boy kept his eyes glued to the entrance to the glen. Suddenly there was a gleam as the sun caught the steel of gun-barrels and swords. John stayed only long enough to make sure the soldiers' coats were red, then he was away like a hare over the heather to the cottage below. The gentlemen were still there, standing by their horses. John's sister, Morag, was carrying cups of water and oatcakes to them when John burst into the yard.

'The Redcoats are turning up the glen!' he cried.

The gentlemen sprang toward their horses. 'How long before they are here?' they asked.

'They have more than five miles to ride over a bad road. Perhaps twenty minutes, perhaps a little longer,' John's father, Donald Cameron, told them.

'Can you lead us to the coast?' a tall man asked him. 'We hope to find a ship there to take the Prince to France.'

'The only way is up the glen and over the mountains. You would be seen as you crossed the bare hills.'

'We shall have to chance that . . .' the

38

Prince began, when Morag broke in – 'Sir, if you will listen a minute, I have a plan. It might be safer if you stayed here.'

'Here, with the enemy's soldiers at our heels?' cried the tall man.

But the Prince held up his hand for silence. 'Let us hear what the little lass has to say.'

'Sir, you are much the same height and appearance as our elder brother, Ewan. He tends the sheep and cattle on the hill. I could fit you out with a kilt and sheepskin coat like his and you could take his place. Our brother will find somewhere to hide in the hills.' She turned to her father. 'The soldiers must know the Prince has ridden this way. If you take his horse and lead the gentlemen up the glen, they will think he is with you.'

'But what will happen when they catch up with us and find the Prince is not there?' the tall man asked.

'We shall reach the other side of the ridge before they can catch up with us,' Donald Cameron told him. 'There you must leave your horses and go on foot to a cave I know near the top of Carn Mor. You can hide there till it is safe to go on to the coast.'

'Leave our horses?' one man cried in dismay.

'He's right! The horses are worn out and will not carry us much longer,' the tall man said. 'And the enemy will be scouring the roads for a bunch of horsemen. They won't be looking for men on foot. They can't bring their horses up the mountain either. But where shall we hide our horses?'

'There is a quarry at the far side of a wood in a cleft in the hills,' Donald Cameron told them.

'How will the Prince join us again?' another man asked.

Donald Cameron nodded toward John. 'My lad has been with the sheep all his life. He knows every track among the hills. He will bring the Prince to you at the cave on Carn Mor.'

'It is a simple plan that I think might work,' the Prince declared. 'I am willing to trust my life to these people.'

'We have no time to lose,' Morag said. 'Take His Highness to the bedroom, John, and I will bring the kilt and sheep-skin coat to you there.' She turned to the men. 'They belonged to our eldest brother James who died in battle at Falkirk,' she said, 'But I know he would have been proud that the Prince should wear them.'

'Come, gentlemen! We must ride hard to reach the ridge,' Donald Cameron said. 'If the soldiers ask you where I am, Morag, you are to tell them I have gone to look for lost cattle in Glen Dessary.' He swung into the saddle and the troop of riders were away up the glen, with the tall man leading the Prince's horse.

John and Morag waited in the kitchen while the Prince put on the garments.

'If you tell the soldiers my father has gone up Glen Dessary you will be telling them a *lie*,' John whispered.

'I will word it so that I am not telling a lie,' Morag replied quickly. 'Listen, John! When the soldiers come they will ask you questions, too. You must not give the Prince away to them.'

'But I promised James I would never tell a lie,' John reminded her.

'James died fighting for the Prince in battle. Remember that!' Morag whispered fiercely. 'If you betray the Prince to the Redcoats, don't think that I or any of the Camerons will ever forgive you.'

'A promise should never be broken,' John said stubbornly. 'But if you can

word your answer to them so that you don't tell a lie, then I can, too!'

Before Morag could reply the Prince appeared from the bedroom, dressed in the sheepskin coat and kilt. He was carrying his fine tartan jacket and velvet breeches over his arm.

'We must get rid of those!' Morag said at once. 'If the soldiers search the house and find them they will know you are not far away. None of our men wear such fine clothes as these. Push them inside your coat, John, and give them to Ewan to hide behind the waterfall.' She looked again at the Prince. 'You are much too *clean* for a herdsman. Come outside and let me smear your hands and face with mud. You must get the dirt under your fingernails too, or your hands will give you away as a gentleman.'

When this was done she gave the Prince his last instructions. 'Listen, Sir! Ewan is *dumb*. That's well known about here. So whatever the soldiers do or say, you must not speak. When you see them nearing the house, come down the hill driving the cattle before you. It will seem natural, as it will be the time to milk the cows, and they will never think a cowherd could be the Prince. John will take you now to Ewan. Then come quickly home, John. You must be back here before the Redcoats arrive!'

The Prince and John sped up the hillside while Morag went into the bedroom to make sure the Prince had left nothing behind. There, on a chair, was his wig! All the gentlemen wore grand wigs, she knew – but not the farm workers!

'Oh, I must get rid of that quickly!' cried Morag. She snatched up a pair of scissors. 'Into the tub of dye along with the sheep's wool!' She snipped the curls

of the wig into pieces and plunged them into the dye. Then she sat down at the spinning wheel and tried to steady herself by spinning the wool. It was not long before John came leaping down the hill and ran, breathless, into the kitchen.

'The Prince is with the cattle?' asked Morag anxiously.

John nodded.

'And Ewan? Where is he?'

'He's gone to the cave behind the water-fall.'

'He understands what you told him?'

'Yes. He gave the Prince his shepherd's crook.'

At that moment they heard the sound of horses' hoofs.

'They're coming! Remember! Watch your tongue!' Morag whispered.

'If I can't answer them without telling a lie, then I'll stay silent,' John replied.

Morag had no chance to argue. The Redcoats came bursting through the door without so much as knocking. They stopped, surprised to find a young girl quietly spinning while her brother stirred the tub of dye.

'What have we here? A couple of children? Where's your mother?' the Captain of the Redcoats demanded.

Morag stopped spinning. 'Dead these two years, sir.'

'And your father?'

'He said he was going up Glen Dessary to look for a lost cow,' answered Morag. 'That's the next glen to the north,' she added, and glanced quickly at John.

'Is that the truth, my lad?' the Captain snapped.

'That is what my father said, sir,' John replied. 'Well,' he thought to himself, 'he did *say* he was going there.'

'Have you seen horsemen along this road?' the Captain asked.

'Why, yes, sir!' Morag replied. She knew the Redcoats must have seen the hoof-marks in the mud.

'Was Prince Charles one of them?'

'There was one of them *looked* like a Prince. He was wearing a fine tartan jacket and velvet breeches and a wig,' John put in before Morag could reply.

'That sounds like the Prince. Which way did they go?'

'The horsemen went up the glen,' said Morag.

'And where would that take them?' the Captain asked.

'They could come to Loch Morar,' Morag replied. 'Or it might be they took the path to Loch Nevis.'

'Did you see them do that?' The Captain's voice was sharp.

Morag shook her head. 'We can't see round the bend in the road from the house. But our brother Ewan might have seen them from the hill.'

'So you have another brother? Why is he not here?'

This time John answered. 'Ewan is our shepherd and herdsman, sir. He goes up to the hill pasture with the sheep and cattle.'

'Then fetch him down here at once,' the Captain ordered.

'Oh, sir, my brother can't tell you anything. He's dumb,' said Morag. 'He might understand you, but he couldn't reply.'

The Captain looked as if he did not believe Morag.

'Bring him here all the same. We will

put some questions to him,' he said.

One of his men spoke up. 'What the lass says is true, sir. I have lived all my life at Fort William and I have heard men speak of "Cameron's Dumbie." Isn't that him, coming down the hillside now, behind the cows?' he asked Morag.

Morag did not answer the question directly. Instead she said, 'It is time for the cows to be milked. Go and hurry him down, John.'

'While we are waiting you can search the cottage,' the Captain told his men. 'Look hard for any trace that the Prince has been here.'

The men searched, but they found nothing.

'What's in this evil-looking tub?' the Captain asked.

'It holds the heather dye that I steep my wool in before I spin it,' Morag told him. The Captain poked his sword in the tub and Morag held her breath and prayed that the curls of the wig had taken on the dye like the sheep's wool. Luckily, before the Captain noticed anything John came into the room with the Prince. All depended now on whether the Prince could hold his tongue and whether John could match his wits to the Captain's and

still not tell a lie.

'Now, Ewan, there is a rich reward for anyone who helps us catch the Prince. Did you see him riding up the glen with his horsemen?'

The Prince made no answer.

'My brother is a bit deaf, too,' said John.

The Captain bellowed again. 'Did you see the horsemen riding up the glen? Nod your head or shake it, can't you?'

This time the Prince nodded his head.

'Did they turn right or left over the hills, or did they go straight on?'

The Prince let his jaw fall open as if he were witless. Morag went through a pantomime of pointing right and left and straight before her. The Prince copied her movements carefully.

'Mercy on us! He's daft as well as dumb!' the Captain cried in a temper. He gave the Prince a blow on the head. 'Shut your silly mouth!' he snapped.

Morag and John held their breath. But the Prince merely shut his mouth and hung his head.

'He's got no more sense than his cattle! We're wasting our time here while the Prince gets farther away up the glen. Go back to your cows, you idiot! To your horses, men!'

The Redcoats turned and ran out into the yard. The Prince and the children watched them. Then, when they were out of sight, all three began to laugh.

'The clever way you answered their questions saved my life,' said the Prince.

'But you were clever too, sir. You kept your temper when the Captain struck you and spoke so rudely,' Morag told him.

'Anyway, we none of us told a lie,' John said happily.

Morag explained about John's promise.

'Were you not tempted to tell who I was when the Captain spoke of the reward?' asked the Prince.

'Not for all the riches in the world! You are *our* Prince,' declared Morag.

That night John led the Prince by secret paths to the cave where his men were hiding. Then he and his father tramped back home across the heather hills. For two days the Prince and his friends hid in the cave. Then they made their way to the seashore where they found a boatman who took them to the islands for safety. Many months later a French ship came to carry the Prince to France. He never went back to Scotland again, but John and Morag never forgot him, and he would remember them.

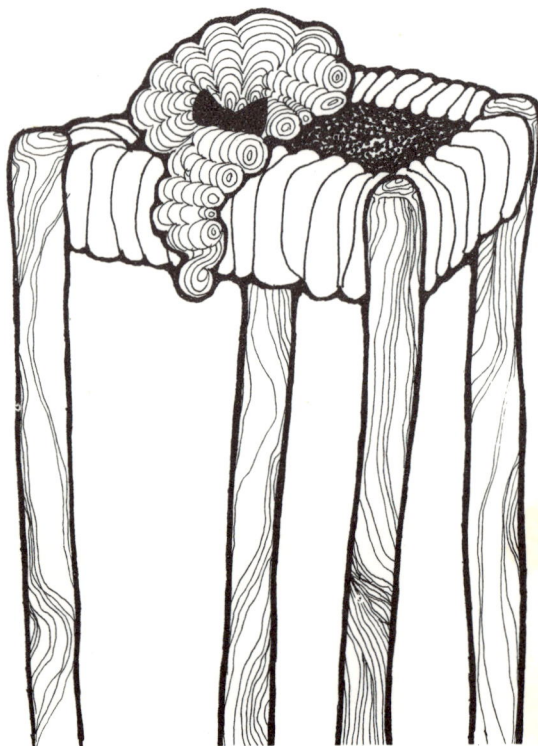

CARING FOR YOUR PETS

If you would like to keep a pet, there is one thing you must remember. A pet is not a toy to be forgotten the moment you are bored with it. Your pet depends on you, so it is up to you to make sure that it is properly fed, has enough to drink, the space and exercise it needs, and that its home is kept clean.

Before you decide to have a pet, think hard. Are you prepared to spend time every day looking after it? Is there someone you can trust to take care of your pet for you when you go away on vacation? It would be very cruel to neglect your pet, and if you are not sure you could look after it, then you ought not to keep one at all.

Once you are sure you are the right person to keep a pet, you still have to decide what kind you would like. When you are thinking about this, ask yourself some more questions. How much space is there in your home? Are there any public parks or fields nearby? How much can you spend on food for your pet? Is there nearly always someone at home, or is the house empty most of the day?

It is very important to think of all these things. If you bought a puppy, for instance, and then found there was nowhere for you to exercise it properly, no one at home during the day to keep it company, and that it grew into an enormous dog with an enormous appetite and you didn't have enough pocket money to buy meat every day, you would end up with a very unhappy, unhealthy pet. It is much better to keep a happy goldfish than an unhappy Alsatian.

Once you have decided which is the best pet for you to keep, find out as much as you can about its needs and habits. You can borrow books about keeping pets from libraries, and most pet shops sell pamphlets which tell you exactly how to care for each type of pet. Learn all you can about your chosen pet. Then you can be sure that when it arrives it will soon settle happily into its new home.

If, when you have thought about it, you decide you haven't enough space for a big pet, don't be too disappointed. A smaller pet can become just as much your friend as a big one.

A hamster takes up very little space, and is not expensive to feed. It still needs looking after carefully, of course. You must make sure it has the right type and size of cage, and one that is easy to clean. The cage should be kept in a warm place, and you will have to put sawdust on the floor of the cage and hay for bedding. Only one hamster should be kept in a cage, as these animals quarrel and fight when they live together.

Hamsters are 'nocturnal' animals. This means they sleep most of the day and wake up at night. But as a hamster grows used to its owner it often becomes more lively during the day and enjoys being handled. It is important to know how to pick up a hamster. Never lift one when it is asleep.

Other pets you could keep which are similar to the hamster are white mice, guinea pigs, and gerbils.
Pick it up when it is facing you, and close your hand over the top of the body so that it can't bite or jump out of your hand.

If you keep a hamster you will need to feed it once a day in the evening. Hamsters should have some hard food each day to gnaw on, but never anything sharp which might injure their pouches. They also like scraps of meat, cooked egg, fish, bacon rind, cheese, lettuce, raw carrot and other root vegetables, and peanuts. They love milk, but there should always be some water left in their cages, too.

If you put a wheel in a hamster's cage it will get plenty of exercise running on the rungs. A hamster will enjoy climbing ladders in the cage, too, and if there is a good piece of hard wood there it will always have something to gnaw on.

A parakeet is another pet you can think about keeping if you haven't much room. You will need as big a cage as you can afford, with perches set at different heights so that the parakeet has enough exercise. He should have some toys—a bell, mirror and ladder—to amuse him. There should be sandpaper and a layer of gravel on the floor of the cage, and these must be changed about every two days.

You can feed a parakeet quite cheaply on bird seed bought from a pet shop. He also needs greens such as chickweed, chicory, or lettuce, a cuttlefish bone, and fresh water every day. When a parakeet has grown used to his new home he will love to come out of his cage into the room. But make sure that all the doors and windows are closed before you let out a bird.

If you want to train a parakeet to talk, only one person should talk to him. The 'trainer' should start with just one word, repeating it every time he goes to the bird. Not all parakeets can be trained, so don't be too disappointed if yours never learns.

You can keep goldfish in the smallest home, either in a bowl or a tank. If you are using a bowl, remember that it shouldn't be filled to the top with water. There must be enough water surface for the goldfish to have plenty of air. There should be a little gravel in the bottom of the bowl, and a few floating plants.

If you are keeping goldfish in a tank, you will also need to put gravel at the bottom. You can put plants and rocks in the tank, too, but you should first find out what type to use. Special rocks for fish tanks can be bought at pet shops. Don't use a rock or stone you have found

in the garden. It may have rough edges which can damage the fish, and it could poison the water, too.

Feeding a goldfish is very simple. You can buy dried fish food mixture from pet shops. Be careful not to overfeed goldfish. Uneaten food will rot at the bottom of the tank or bowl and poison the water.

These are just a few of the smaller pets you can keep. If you do decide to have a hamster, parakeet or goldfish, remember that what you have read here is only a guide to show you how much thought, work and care each one needs, and to help you make your choice. You should do a lot more 'homework' before you finally buy your pet. Then you can be quite sure that whatever you choose to keep, it will be happy, healthy, and glad that you are its owner – and you will be happy, too.

48